Anonymous

Memorial of Col. Hugh Henry Osgood of Norwich, Conn

Anonymous

Memorial of Col. Hugh Henry Osgood of Norwich, Conn

ISBN/EAN: 9783337723774

Printed in Europe, USA, Canada, Australia, Japan

Cover: Foto ©ninafisch / pixelio.de

More available books at **www.hansebooks.com**

MEMORIAL

OF

Col. Hugh Henry Osgood

OF

NORWICH, CONN.

Record Job Print,
Norwich, Conn

BIOGRAPHICAL SKETCH.

COL. HUGH HENRY OSGOOD, the son of Artemas Osgood and Salome Johnson, was born in Southbridge, Mass., Oct. 10, 1821. His ancestors came to New England in the 17th century. His parents lived later in Pomfret, Conn., and afterwards in Norwich. At an early age he came to Norwich to live with his uncle, Mr. Charles Lee. After two years spent in the schools of the town, he entered the store of Samuel Tyler & Son, where he mastered the details of the drug business. In 1842, when he was 21 years of age, he joined his uncle in founding the house of Lee & Osgood, which has carried on successfully the drug business for nearly sixty years. In this business he placed

3

the first thousand dollars of his earnings, from which grew the large fortune of later years. On the death of his uncle, in 1865, he purchased the entire establishment, and steadily built up the largest and most important drug and chemical business in eastern Connecticut.

A Business Man.

Col. Osgood was first and foremost a business man. His earliest ambition drew him toward business, which chiefly engrossed him. Toward business his strongest activities were directed. Whatever he achieved was the achievement of a business man. He never aspired to eminence except on those heights which a business man could tread. And here his enterprise, resource and energy found ample play. Business he found the school for the training of all the physical, intellectual and moral forces; and the sufficient sphere for the development of the highest integrities. From small beginnings he rose to the foremost rank of the community's captains of industry. His own business specialty prospered not only, but he became associated with larger enterprises in which he was able to place capital and to which he became a guiding and formative influence. To mention them is to call the names of many of the important business concerns of the vicinity and of places more or less remote. He was President of the Uncas Paper Co., The Goodwin Cork Co., The Worcester Thread Co., The Sterling Dyeing and Finishing Co., The Glasgo Yarn Co., The Dime Savings Bank, and the Kitemaug Association. He was one of the early promoters of the Bulletin Co.; for a long period President of the Norwich Bleaching, Dyeing and Printing Co., and when merged into the United States Finishing Co., of New York, was made its Vice President. He was Director of The Thames and First National Banks, of Norwich, The Ashland Cotton Co., of Jewett City, The Norwich Gas and Electric Co., The Yantic Woolen Co., The Richmond Stove Co. He was a Trustee of

5

the Norwich Free Academy, and Treasurer for
forty years of the Central School District. A
simple enumeration of these business connections
reveals the extent and ramifications of his business interests and activities. In the sphere of
business he was resourceful, clear sighted, far
seeing, progressive, cautious, and yet courageous.
He was a wise counsellor to business men seek-
ing guidance. His judgment was constantly
sought, and when given was relied upon. His
sincerity and his integrity were unimpeachable
and universally recognized as unswerving.

A Citizen.

Successful business men are not always good
citizens; they are often self-abstracted and their
interest diverted in selfish directions. Col. Osgood was a good citizen. He interested himself
in the affairs of the community. He sought the
best things for his fellow townsmen. He took
pride in beautifying and making attractive his
adopted city. He went to the sources of its

life and sought to purify them. He was found
in the caucus and the town meeting. He
sought good city government. He gave ten
years to the administration of its affairs as its
Chief Magistrate. He labored for good sanitary
conditions; providing during his administration
the present sewerage system. He helped to
perfect the Fire Department. He was interested
in the city's educational interests, beginning with
its public schools and ending with its Free
Academy. He was interested in its moral con-
dition, and did a full citizen's part in mitiga-
ting its poverty. He was a friend and large
giver to the city's charities; the United Workers
and the City Mission. He took his part in local
politics, insisting on honest methods and honest
men, scorning the tricks of schemers, even when
found in his own party; he was present in the
stormy town meeting, generally its strong, masterful presiding officer, for which service he possessed rare tact and talent. Always exerting an
influence among and over his fellow citizens

which only a strong commanding personality can wield. Where he sat was generally the head of the table. No wonder that when he was being borne to his last resting place, his fellow citizens with remarkable unanimity closed their stores, banks and places of business to express their great sense of loss; for though Norwich has had many noble citizens, few have wrought so extensively and so unselfishly for her welfare.

A Patriot.

If Col. Osgood was a public spirited citizen in his adopted city, he was none the less a devoted patriot and lover of his country. He had a broad, comprehensive and accurate grasp of public and national questions. His easy comprehension of national issues; his judgment of public men; his forecast of political events and issues were phenomenal. Nothing in the movement of national life escaped his eye. No man excelled him in his desire to see the wise and

8

just thing done for the whole country. If he was a politician he used his party as the instrument of service to his country. He wanted to see his country great, and was in sympathy with all that looked toward the expansion of its resources and its power of service to the world. He was deeply interested in the slavery question and was one of the original founders of the Republican party. He was a delegate in 1855 to the convention held in Hartford of that year, which inaugurated the movement which created the Republican party. During the Civil War he was active and pronounced in his support of the Union. He was a member of Gov. Buckingham's staff during his administration, and was entrusted by the great war Governor with important missions for the state and the nation. He was foremost in efforts for the support of the government; was a member of the Loyal League, formed to promote the interests of the Union cause. Col. Osgood was always unwilling to accept political office, but he was a distinct political force to be counted upon and to be reckoned with, and a potential factor in political affairs. His influence in the state and beyond it, was felt and recognized; and because it was unselfish and patriotic it was all the more effective.

A Christian.

Col. Osgood was a Christian. He inherited Christian traditions; was reared in a Christian atmosphere, and became a professor of the Christian faith. He was a member of the Park Congregational Church from its organization and previously of the Second Congregational Church, from which the new church was formed. He was a believer of the cardinal doctrines of Christianity, and believed them strongly. He was a Christian without cant and without ostentation. His religion was healthy, sane, sustaining. Not as much on his lips as on those of some others, but when not expressed, yet in solution in all he did. He was practical in his

Christianity. It prompted him to bear the burdens of others and to help in the dead lift. He gave largely of his time and his money to religious work. He helped the man in need. No one knew the utmost reach of his beneficence, for he gave without ostentation and did what he could to keep his philanthropy from public observation. His church and the city's charities, Christian missions, and educational institutions were enriched by his practical beneficence. Without intruding it agressively upon others, he carried his religion into the home, into the circles of friendship, into his business, into his politics, and to all those points of touch which he maintained with his fellow men.

In the Home.

He was best loved by those who came nearest to him. He was by nature genial and affectionate. He had a genius for friendship, and few men were more warmly loved by friends whom he had bound to himself by enduring bonds. Thoughtfulness and kindness characterized his relations to relatives and family, before knowing the closer bond which came later in life. On June 23, 1892, he was married to Miss Mary Ruth Lee, of Manlius, New York; a union that brought new joy and comfort to his later years. And so in strength and vigor of powers which showed nothing of waning to the last, he lived his full round of life till on the 22nd of October, 1899, at Manlius, New York, death laid his gentle hand upon him and he slept, leaving a great void, filled once and for long by a gracious and inspiring personality.

FUNERAL ADDRESS

Delivered at Park Church by the Pastor.

THERE is no finer gift of Providence to a
community than the gift of a great citizen.
The noblest product of our modern life, the
best expression of the modern spirit is a strong,
human life devoted to the interests and best
welfare of its fellow men; its fellow townsmen;
its country; the kingdom of God; the world.
Good citizenship has its roots in the home; in
the practice of the domestic fidelities; it roots
itself in the community, taking thought and
time for the happiness, the well being and the
advancement of the people of the vicinage. It
is public spirited and alert to the interests of

13

its fellow citizens. It is patriotic; it takes its country to its heart; what it thinks of the republic, according to the Roman maxim, is written on its forehead. And lastly, good citizenship is religious; it has faith in God, the Righteous Ruler and Judge of men, and does all its work beneath the Taskmaker's eye. It fronts the home, the community, the country and kingdom of God; and takes duty to humanity wherever need exists. Judged by these criteria, this man was a great citizen. And this style of an all round man, a fully rounded out character, is the noblest work of God. It is not essential to great citizenship that high official station be reached, or that conspicuous offices be filled; it is sufficient that such stations be deserved, rather than occupied. It is to the high credit of this man that he could have had every office which an ambitious man might have asked, from the governorship of his state down; but that, declining everything offered and pressed in his direction, he only asked to be a private citizen in his adopted town, serving his fellow townsmen and his fellow countrymen, his church and his God from the common walks of life. Every one of you knows that no office in his reach could have brought him added honor. The few offices of responsibility or trust which his fellow townsmen thrust upon him added nothing to the name he won, and were only accepted as the means of rendering his city a needed service. You and I, with the utmost stretch of our imaginations, could not conceive this man reaching after any kind of official station for the sake of its emoluments or its honor. He was absolutely innocent of this sort of personal ambition, a statement that needs to be made in the interest of that wide reach of influence exerted by him in total disconnection from any sort or suggestion of officialism. He was a great citizen, notwithstanding the fact that the base of his influence was neither in Hartford nor Washington, although his influence was potent enough to easily reach each of those cities. It is a fine thing to stand apart from the adventitious helps of every form of officialism and by the sheer force of a strong and magnetic personality to command the respect and admiration of one's fellow men, and even sway them with a kind of regality of influence that all of us bow before. No man has ever lived in this community who better illustrates the potency of simple, undecorated character. He wore no insignia and bore no official badges or outward decorations that were other than nominal, and yet he exerted an influence in this community that touched in some way nearly every one who has lived in our city. No man was ever more thoroughly identified with every form of helpful, uplifting activity in the community. No man has done more to lift the moral tone of the city to a higher key. And he has done this by what he was, and by what he did. He was strong by nature, no doubt ; some of the best granite went into his original makeup. The best things in the older

generations seemed to have been passed over
to him.   He inherited the Puritan instinct. He
must have been born with a fine sense of jus-
tice and righteousness.   His scorn of meanness
and hypocrisy he must have brought with him
into life, since it is uncommon to see men so
successfully cultivate it as an exotic.   His reverence for right and sacred things ; his venera-
tion for truth ; his keen, moral sense, which
drew the separating seam sharp and clear between right and wrong, appeared native to the
soil of his nature ; so that we wonder some-
times if he was ever tempted along these ethi-
cal lines where other men falter and fall.   We
doubt if he ever debated these moral questions,
so instant was his gravitation toward the right.
It was a man of this moral fibre, holding himself to these fine ideals of manhood, who turned
toward his fellow townsmen and to his fellow men everywhere eager to serve them.   It
is what men are that is their chief equipment
for service ; giving power and projectile force to

what they do. "What you are," said Emerson, "speaks so loudly that I fail to hear what you say." It was this in our noble friend that impressed us. It was the mass and the fineness of his personality that gave him that potent influence among us. It was what he was in his own right and what he did with strong, masterful hand that gave him that singular power of leadership that made him so commanding in his influence. He did not arrogate the right to command men, yet no man ever had among us a larger or a more loyal following. He had that undefinable power of influence that made men glad to go the way he was going. We confided in him; we trusted him; we took his counsel, glad to get our bearings from him when we were uncertain of our guiding stars. How well he was furnished for this! How resourceful he was; what ready grasp of perplexing situations; what clarity of vision; what solidity of judgment characterized his verdict when he had thought through these questions of business, politics, charity, churchmanship that were incessantly submitted to him. His intellectual and moral sanity were phenomenal. How often we have wondered at the ease with which he carried large and complicated business interests; the facility with which he bore heavy burdens for himself and for others and yet met you with a patrician grace and courtesy which made you think he had not a care or an anxiety in the world. What a royal friend he was, so independent and self-sufficing that none of us could help him; though all of us could be sure of a helping hand for the dead lift that was upon ourselves. How he trusted men, believed in them, made them better and stronger men for the confidence he placed in them. Few men surpassed him in keen, discriminating knowledge of men; no man hated baseness or falsity with a sharper indignation, and yet he trusted men; like Thomas Arnold, he made men noble by believing in them. It was this that made his friendship a cherished and coveted boon. I can-

19

not withold my admiration for the men who have stood around Colonel Osgood through many decades, holding their place in his affection, confidence and warm friendship. And for these men who have been associated with him in his business for one, two, three decades, his trusted employees, holding their place in his confidence through so many years of service, for them I have the heartiest and most sincere felicitations. It is an unimpeachable certificate of character to have held through these years the confidence and high regard of such a man. It was because Colonel Osgood was such a man as this and served this community with such continuous and immeasurable service that his going lays such a heavy weight upon our hearts. We have good men still, but we have not his like, I fear, left among us. We scarcely know how to go on without him; the wheels of our life seem as if brought to a sudden standstill. A gaping vacancy stares us in the face. We can easily doubt if Norwich ever lost in

one stroke so much; for whatever other men
among us have wrought on the wider fields of
action, this man was mortised in the whole life
of the city. Life has been made a worthier
thing to all of us because he has lived and
wrought so largely, so wisely and so helpfully
here. He gave himself completely to Norwich.
And so we feel our loss. The uprooting of
this big tree seems to have loosened the soil
in all our little gardens. We all must feel that
we must do more now than we have done, and
be larger in the girth of our manhood,
or the loss will be remediless. We have
seen many noble men drop at our side here,
for Norwich has been rich in better than Spar-
tan blood, and now we must add one more
name to the list of the noble dead. Almost
the noblest Roman of them all. And of them,
together with him, I wish to speak one admon-
itory word to these men of Norwich before I
close. There are chosen names of noble men
who have lived in our city which are recalled to

us on all public occasions; names that ring like bells in our ears as the years go by; and to that chime of bells we must now add another name which we shall hear if Norwich continues to remember her true benefactors. These names are recalled to us for one definite reason; it is this : These men of whom we hear so frequently and will continue to hear, allied themselves intimately with the things that make Norwich great as they make any city great. And those great things are our educational institutions, our Christian churches, our noble charities, our public libraries and the high standards and recognized canons of conduct which hold men to commercial honor and civic purity. We perpetuate the memory of no man who disconnects himself from any of these things which make a city great or a community sweet and pure. These men whom we commemorate are men who made the churches strong; they made provision for the education of the people through the schools and the public libraries; they poured a steady stream of benevolence into the channels of the city's charities and they strove to lift the standard of commercial honor and civic life in the community. It was these great things that made them great; and by standing well in with these they will make us great; but stand apart from these things and Norwich will bury you and speedily forget that you ever lived within her corporate limits. Colonel Osgood stood by all these forces which make for great civic and communal life, and Norwich will only cease to remember him when she ceases to be true to her noblest traditions and false to her loftiest precedents.

The Court of Common Council

OF THE
City of Norwich

HON. HUGH H. OSGOOD,

FOR MANY YEARS OUR MAYOR

and always a public-spirited and enterprising citizen of our community. We shall miss from the accustomed places of trade, finance and public affairs, and the various walks of life, a dignified and imposing figure, and an able and influential actor and adviser.

Hugh H. Osgood was a man of outspoken views and decisive action. Sagacious and self-reliant, with recognized integrity and sound judgment, his fellow citizens were drawn to him for counsel and advice. He zealously aided them with his wisdom, experience, influence and not infrequently out of his means. Whenever he took a position with or for his friends, as occasion often happened he never swerved in fidelity, or relaxed in steadfastness.

Hugh H. Osgood gave to our City government his best services, he gave to his party the wisest counsel, he gave to his country unflinching loyalty, and he gave to his fellow men unbroken friendship. These strong and useful traits made their impress on the people, and, though he was not in official place, they nevertheless, at all times looked upon

RESOLVED.

Resolutions of Respect

of Various Organizations with which Colonel Osgood
held connections.

New England Drug Exchange.

It is with great sorrow that we learn of the death
of our friend and former President, HUGH H. OSGOOD,
who has been associated with us for so many years. To
each member of our association he had become a personal friend, and each feels a personal loss in his decease.

His strict integrity, uniform courtesy and good judgment commanded the respect and admiration of all who
knew him.

He has left us an example which we shall do well to
follow — "What the character of a business man should
be." It has been well said of him that he was "A good
citizen, and stood for all that was best in the community."

Respected and honored as he was among us, we can
appreciate in some measure how much he was beloved by
those intimately connected with him, and how great their
loss is.

We would extend to them our sincere sympathy in their sorrow, and may they be comforted and strengthened as they look back upon his life of usefulness, and the good he accomplished here, and forward to that re-union which we trust awaits us all in the home beyond.

Voted, That a copy of the above testimonial be spread upon our records, and be forwarded to the family and business associates.

JOHN A. GILMAN,
CHARLES F. CUTLER, } *Committee.*
WILLIAM O. BLANDING,

Norwich Board of Trade.

At a meeting of the executive committee of the Norwich Board of Trade, held Tuesday, the following minutes were unanimously adopted, and it was voted that a page of the records be devoted to them, together with a history of the late Hon. Hugh H. Osgood's connection with the board, and that copies be transmitted to his family.

The death of Hugh Henry Osgood removes from the membership of the Board of Trade one to whose influence and efforts this organization owes, in great measure, the prosperity, activity and usefulness which marked the earliest years of its existence. As its first president for two successive years his name alone, standing, as it has always stood, for integrity, honor, intelligence and ability of the highest order, gave to our organization a dignity and influence which insured its standing in the community. And when, in addition to this silent influence, we had the full benefit of his wise and broad-minded direction of our affairs, freely given at the cost of his valuable time, and his remarkable energy, in a spirit of patriotic devotion to the public good, we feel that no tribute which we can pay to his memory will adequately express our appreciation of his official relation to our board.

If we cannot expect, through the poor medium of words, to express ourselves for our organization alone, much less can we hope to express the personal esteem in which our late fellow member was held in the community. As a type of the truest Christian manliness he will live in our memory, leaving with us an influence of patriotic citizenship, liberal philanthropy, spotless integrity and loyal friendship which will be sacredly cherished as the only compensation for the loss which is profoundly impressed upon us in his removal from our midst.

A. R. ABORN, *President*.

GEORGE S. SMITH, *Secretary*.

The Dime Savings Bank.

At a meeting of the directors of The Dime Savings Bank, held Monday, Oct. 23, the following minute was unanimously adopted :

The directors of The Dime Savings Bank wish to place upon its records a tribute to the memory of its late president, Hugh H. Osgood, and to express their

27

deep personal sorrow at the loss of one who took an active and leading part in its organization and in all its subsequent history.

Mr. Osgood was one of the original incorporators of the bank and was chosen a vice president at its first meeting, held in 1869. Upon the death of Mr. Edward R. Thompson, the first president, who held office until September, 1897, he was elected his successor, and accepted the office with the simple yet prophetic words: "I thank you, gentlemen, but I can serve you only a little while."

Amid a multiplicity of cares and demands upon his attention he gave unremittingly to the bank of his time, his strength and of that clear judgment and quick insight which made him pre-eminently a valued counsellor in public and private affairs.

He combined in a marked degree those qualities of head and heart which made him not only a leader of men but a genial companion whom it was a delightful privilege to meet week after week; and our sense of personal bereavement is not less than the loss the bank has sustained.

He commanded the confidence and respect of every one who met him, and he will be mourned by the entire community, as well as by his business associates.

We respectfully tender our heartfelt sympathy to the family of our late president in their bereavement.

As a further evidence of our respect the bank will be closed during the hours of the funeral and the directors will attend the services in a body.

F. L. WOODARD, *Secretary*.

The Thames National Bank.

At a meeting of the board of directors of The Thames National Bank of Norwich, Oct. 24, 1899, called to take action upon the death of their fellow director, Hon. Hugh H. Osgood, the following minute was adopted and ordered to be spread upon the records:

By the death of the Hon. Hugh H. Osgood there is lost to the state and community a patriotic and public spirited citizen of the best type; to our business interests an exemplar of enterprise, thrift and honorable conduct of affairs; to the poor a friend ever sympathizing, helpful and generous.

Full of years and honors, he has gone to his rest with the respect, the esteem and the love of all by whom he was known. No man has been more widely identified with all the varied interests of a community, with its political and social life, its churches and schools, its manufacturing, mercantile and financial enterprises; and in all he was a leader, not by reason of self-seeking, but by the common consent of his fellows, who have recognized in him a superiority in wisdom, in self control, in tact and disinterestedness.

Kindly in heart and genial in bearing, he invited confidence, and, from the stores of his large experience, gave counsel to the inexperienced or perplexed. No measure for the public welfare, no plan to relieve private distress but enlisted his ready sympathy and active assistance.

29

Always progressive, he kept pace with the advance of the age, and in appreciation of every material improvement in social, scientific and industrial affairs he was as one entering upon a career and desirous of equipping himself with the best instruments of success. Large minded and far seeing, he wrought for the best interests of the community in which he lived, and among the successful institutions of his town there are few which do not bear the impress of his energy, knowledge and public spirit.

In voicing its own severe loss, this board joins in sympathy with a community which is bereaved of its foremost citizen.

Voted, That this banking house be closed during the hours of the funeral and that the directors attend the services in a body.

CHAS. W. GALE, *Cashier.*

The First National Bank.

At a meeting of the directors of The First National Bank, held Oct. 25, the following action was had:

The death of Hon. Hugh H. Osgood has fallen upon the community with suddenness, with almost paralyzing force. On every side spontaneous expressions of respect and affection are heard, and sincere regret that this community has lost its first citizen.

No eulogistic expression can completely portray his character, which had for its broad foundation truth, honor and integrity and all those characteristics which marked the moral, the social, the religious and the business life of an upright man.

He was in touch with and his force was felt in business enterprises to an extent that is the possibility of few men only. He yielded his personal comfort and pleasure at the solicitation of friends, who leaned upon him in association for advice and assistance. In business his was notably the strong arm.

In church and school, and in all the walks of life, he was an intelligent, sympathetic and strong leader, the supporter of all that is good and true.

In charities the kindliest sympathies and the generous impulses of a Christian philanthropist took expression in the deeds done, the number of which none can know.

Joining in the universal expression of sorrow, and in sympathy and love for a true friend, this board desires to record their appreciation of the man, and their pleasure in having so long enjoyed his friendship and association, as well as his valuable advice and co-operation in its affairs.

It is further ordered that the bank be closed on the afternoon of Thursday, Oct. 26th, and that the directors attend the funeral services.

F. S. JEROME, *Cashier.*

The Norwich Savings Society.

At a special meeting of the directors of The Norwich Savings Society, held Oct. 25, the following minute was adopted:

31

In expression of the sympathy entertained by this board of the loss sustained by the community in the death of the Hon. Hugh H. Osgood, and that we may the last tribute of respect and esteem to the memory of our distinguished fellow citizen:

Voted, That the banking house of The Norwich Savings Society be closed at 1 P. M. on the 26th day of October, 1899, and that the directors and employees attend the funeral services.

JOHN MITCHELL, *President.*

The Uncas Paper Company.

At a meeting of the board of directors of The Uncas Paper Company, held Oct. 25, 1899, called to take action upon the death of their president, Honorable Hugh H. Osgood, the following minute was adopted and ordered to be spread upon the records:

By the death of the Honorable Hugh H. Osgood, this company has lost one of its original incorporators, a director from its inception and its president for the past two years.

We bear testimony to the strength and simplicity of his character; to the kindly grace of his social bearing; to his successful business abilities and irreproachable integrity; to the generous helpfulness of his nature, and to all those shining attributes that distinguished him as the possessor of a true and honorable manhood.

He gave unremittingly to this company of his time,

32

his strength and all that clear judgment and quick insight that made him a most valuable counsellor in the affairs of the company.

Kindly in heart and genial in bearing, he had the confidence and respect of every one who met him; and he will be mourned by the entire community as well as by his intimate associates.

With these sentiments sincerely entertained in the hearts of the directors they have

Resolved, To inscribe this expression upon the records of the company and to insert a copy of the same in the Norwich daily papers.

Voted, That the mill be closed during the hours of the funeral in order that the employees may attend the services.

F. W. BROWNING, *Secretary*.

The Masonic Temple Corporation.

At a meeting of the directors of The Masonic Temple Corporation, held in Masonic Temple Monday evening, the following minute and vote were unanimously passed:

While Hon. H. H. Osgood, 32°, was not a director, nor even an incorporator, of this corporation, it is felt that his death should receive something more than a passing notice from us. In spite of the almost innumerable interests, public, corporate and private, which demanded his attention, he took a deep interest in the formation and success of this corporation, subscribing

33

liberally for our bonds, willingly consenting to act as trustee for the bondholders, in which capacity his autograph appears upon all the bonds.

He was ever ready, with his mature judgment, to give us the benefit of his vast experience at the time of our organization and later in the conduct of affairs, and the success which has attended the corporation was a source of deep gratification to him.

It is therefore Voted, That a page in the records of this corporation be set apart to the memory of Hon. Hugh Henry Osgood, the upright citizen, the incorruptible public official, the firm and devoted friend, in short, the consistent Mason, with all that is implied thereby.

Official: ARTHUR H. BREWER, *President.*
CHAS. B. CHAPMAN, *Secretary.*

Hugh H. Osgood Lodge, I. O. O. F., M. U.

At a special meeting of Hugh H. Osgood Lodge, I. O. O. F., M. U., held in their rooms Oct. 23, 1899, the following resolutions were adopted:

In view of the loss we have sustained by the decease of our friend and honorary member, the Honorable Hugh H. Osgood, and the still heavier loss sustained by those who were nearest and dearest to him, be it

Resolved, That it is only a just tribute to the memory of the departed to say that in regretting his removal from our midst we mourn for one who was in every way worthy of our respect and regard.

Resolved, That we sincerely condole with the family of the deceased on the dispensation with which it has pleased Divine Providence to afflict them, and commend them for consolation to Him who orders all things for the best and whose chastisements are meant in mercy.

Resolved, That this heartfelt testimonial of our sympathy and sorrow be forwarded to the family of our departed friend, and that a copy be entered on the records of our lodge; also published in the Morning Bulletin and the Norwich Evening Record.

P. G. ROBERT MCNEELY, ⎫ *Committee*
P. G. EDWARD CROOKS, ⎬ *on*
P. S. JOHN GRAY, ⎭ *Resolutions.*

Wauregan Steam Fire Engine Company.

At a special meeting of the Wauregan Steam Fire Engine Company, No. 1, held Tuesday, Oct. 24, 1899, the following resolutions were unanimously adopted :

WHEREAS, An All Wise Creator having in His providence removed from our midst our esteemed friend and honorary member, Hon. H. H. Osgood, be it

Resolved, That in his death we lose a trusted friend and adviser, whose memory we shall ever hold in love and reverence.

Resolved, That we tender to the family and friends of the deceased our heartfelt sympathy in their bereavement, and as a mark of our respect for his memory we will drape the front of our house for a period of 30 days.

Resolved, That a copy of these resolutions be transmitted to the family of the deceased, engrossed upon the
records of the company and published.

(Signed)

CALVIN C. WILLIAMS, ⎫
ARCHIBALD S. SPALDING, ⎬ *Committee.*
CHARLES R. BARTLETT, ⎭

Sedgwick Post, No. 1, G. A. R.

At a special meeting of Sedgwick Post, No. 1, Department of Connecticut, G. A. R., held Oct. 24, the following minutes were adopted:

Again death has invaded our ranks and removed
from our midst a beloved comrade of the Citizens' Corps.
In the death of Hon. Hugh H. Osgood this post has
lost not only a member but a friend whose patriotic services, whose loyalty to all that made for the highest
good, whose generous support of the soldiers in the field
as well as the comrades of the Grand Army, and whose
exemplary citizenship entitle his memory to be emblazoned
upon the brightest pages of history.

We acknowledge with gratitude the many acts of
kindness and the material aid received by our post from
him, and we hereby express our sorrow for the great loss
we sustain in the death of so wise and kind a friend.

Therefore we would give a page of records to the
inscriptions of these minutes of our affliction, and extend
to his bereaved family a soldier's deep sympathy.

Norwich Druggists' Association.

A meeting of the Norwich Druggists' Association was held Tuesday, Oct. 24, to consider its inestimable loss in the death of its beloved president, the Hon. H. H. Osgood.

In the death of our associate and president this association not only recognizes its own loss and the personal loss of every one of its members but also the great and incalculable loss to the community, in which he stood a towering and commanding figure.

Voted, That the members of this association close their stores during the hours of the funeral services and attend the services in a body.

> N. D. SEVIN, *Vice President*,
> W. H. NICHOLSON, *Secretary*, } *Committee.*
> JAMES DUGGAN,

The Crescent Fire Arms Company.

At a meeting of the directors of The Crescent Fire Arms Company Wednesday, Oct. 25, 1899, the following minutes were ordered spread upon the records:

We but join the universal expression of grief at the loss sustained by this community in the death of our late co-director, Hon. Hugh Henry Osgood, whose genial presence and pre-eminent capacity have added so much to the pleasure of our meetings and to the success of our business. Colonel Osgood has been an active member of our direction but for a comparatively short period, but

37

even in that time he has proved by act and word his great value to this organization. Therefore we desire to put on record this brief expression of our deep regret at his death.

H. H. GALLUP, *President.*

Ashland Cotton Company.

At a meeting of the directors of the Ashland Cotton Company, of Jewett City, held Friday, Oct. 27, 1899, the following minutes were ordered entered upon the records:

In the death of Hon. Hugh Henry Osgood, for many years a director of this corporation, we deeply feel, both as individuals and as directors, the great loss sustained. The pleasure of our associations at board meetings was very greatly enhanced by the ever genial presence of Colonel Osgood, who possessed to an eminent degree the faculty of giving even to business gatherings an agreeable and social aspect.

In the strictly business relation Colonel Osgood's quick perceptions served to simplify and render clear matters under discussion, and in arriving at conclusions his decided character and vast experience rendered him of the greatest value to this company.

We desire to incorporate among the records of this incorporation our appreciation of the high character, business acumen and agreeable personality of our late associate and of the great loss sustained by ourselves, this company and the entire community in his death.

38

United States Finishing Company.

Upon motion, duly seconded, it was

Voted, That the following tribute be inscribed in the Record Book of the Company, and that a copy be sent to the family of our late Vice President, Col. Hugh H. Osgood :

It becomes a sad privilege of the Directors of this Company to direct that there be inscribed on its Record Book a tribute *in memoriam*, that shall be a testimony and an expression of the deep feeling that touches with pain and sorrow the hearts of his associates, who mourn the death of Vice President Hugh H. Osgood.

We, the Directors of the United States Finishing Company, are sure to miss the strong and guiding assistance that was at our command, and we here unite with the many business and official managements with which he was connected in lamenting the loss of Colonel Osgood as the loss of one amply qualified to bring wise counsel to our deliberations and to assist us in the affairs of the Company with his sound judgment and long experience in our line of work.

We inscribe with profound regret our sense of a bereavement which deprives us of a trustworthy, true and loyal friend.

Sterling Dyeing and Finishing Company.

A special meeting of the Board of Drectors of the Sterling Dyeing and Finishing Company was held on the

39

26th day of October, 1899, to testify to their loss in the death of their late President, Hugh Henry Osgood, when the following minute was adopted and ordered to be spread upon the records of the Company:

The Directors greatly lament the death of Hugh Henry Osgood, who was identified with this Company from its organization, and was one of its original incorporators. He was chosen its President in the early days of said Company, and continued to hold the position until his death. His self control, his mature judgment and ripe experience made him a valuable counsellor in the conduct of the affairs of this Company, and we desire in this brief tribute to his memory to express the respect and esteem in which we hold him in remembrance, and the deep sorrow we feel at his death.

The Board, in order to emphasize their appreciation of the man whose death we mourn and whose loss we keenly feel, order that the mill be closed on the afternoon of his burial, and that the Directors attend the funeral services in a body.

The sincere sympathy of this Company is humbly tendered to the widow and family of the deceased, and the Secretary is requested to transmit a copy of this minute to them.

CLARAMON HUNT, Sec'y.

Central School District.

Minute of the Central School District of Norwich on the death of Col. H. H. Osgood:

In common with the many other organizations of his adopted city, which have been personally and materially affected by the death of Col. H. H. Osgood, the Central School District desires to place on record its sense of the great loss which has befallen it, and its grateful appreciation of his long and faithful service as its Treasurer. For more than forty years Mr. Osgood had managed the financial interests of the District with his well-known ability, probity and fidelity. In all that time he never exacted a cent of salary and never was asked to give a bond. As in all similar positions, the people had faith in his honesty and fidelity, and continued year after year to give him that quiet but emphatic approval — an unanimous election.

Nor did his duties as Treasurer represent all he did for the district. He was frequently resorted to for counsel and advice, and it is believed that no important move has been made in the district within the past forty years without his cognizance and approval. Some men in offices are consulted as a matter of form; courtesy demands it. Not so in Col. Osgood's case. Men had learned to know him and to rely upon his judgment, matured and ripened as it was by such divers and manifold experiences. The death of such a man is a severe loss to any community, and particularly to a community like ours, which was small and compact enough to be touched and influenced on all sides by the manifold interests and activities of his life.

It is in this universal sense of loss and bereavement

that Col. Osgood has reared his own monument. His character and virtues are written in the hearts of his fellow citizens of Norwich.

Resolved, That this minute be spread on the records of the district, and that copies thereof be sent to the widow of Col. Osgood and to the city press for publication.

Young Men's Christian Association of Norwich.

WHEREAS, It has pleased God to take unto Himself our Vice President, Hugh H. Osgood, in whose death the Association suffers the loss of one of its wisest counselors and most valued supporters, and that for many years; and

WHEREAS, This death has occurred in the fulness of his days and in the midst of a life of activity far beyond that accorded the average age of man; therefore be it

Resolved, By the Board of Managers of the Norwich Young Men's Christian Association that, while we join in the general regret at the loss to the community and to us of such a manly man, so staunch a friend, and so firm a supporter of all good causes, yet in our sadness at our loss there comes a note of rejoicing that he was spared so long to the community and to us; that his mental and bodily powers were preserved undiminished to the end; that God has given to our community to possess such a character, the soul of honor, of clean hands and clean lips, with the genius to get and the generosity

42

to give. We are glad to believe that while we shall see his face no more in the flesh, yet the influence of such a life can never die, and posterity will have reason to be thankful for the ideal such a life furnishes. Our sincerest sympathy is extended to his widow and family.

The Bulletin Company.

At a meeting of the Directors of The Bulletin Company the following resolutions of respect were read and adopted:

WHEREAS, Hugh Henry Osgood, our esteemed President, has been removed by death, we hereby express our sorrow and regret that his inestimable services have been brought to an end. By Col. Osgood's death The Bulletin Company has lost an officer whose faithful and efficient services and whose courtesy, ability and judgment have won our respect and admiration.

Resolved, That the sympathy of this Company be conveyed to the widow and family of our deceased President, who, in their deep grief, can only find consolation in the promises of the Master in whom he trusted, and in life sought to honor.

Resolved, That these resolutions be published in The Bulletin, and that a copy be made and signed by the Secretary to be transmitted to the widow of our late President, and that they be made part of the minutes of their meeting and be entered upon the records of The Bulletin Company.

TRIBUTES FROM THE PRESS.

Norwich Record.

In the death of Hon. H. H. Osgood Norwich, as a community, suffers an almost irreparable loss that is universally recognized and sincerely felt. The many large business interests with which he was so long and closely identified are deprived of a wise counsellor, and hundreds of individuals mourn the departure of a personal friend, whose substantial aid has time and again been unostentatiously tendered them.

Col. Osgood was a self-made man who achieved the highest measure of usefulness and influence in both public and private life. He was successful not only in promoting business enterprises, but also in winning by honest and able effort the hearty esteem of his fellow citizens. Firm in his own convictions, he was yet tolerant of opposing opinions, and his advice for years had been sought by men of affairs in all walks of life. His going out creates vacancies many and varied. He will be sadly missed, yet the genuine public sorrow that marks his passage from the scenes of his life-work is mellowed by the realization that his years of activity were prolonged nearly a decade beyond the allotted life of man. His work is done, and the memory of it will long be gratefully cherished by his appreciative townsmen.

Morning Bulletin.

The news of the death of Col. Hugh Henry Osgood carries a feeling of sadness to every department of life with which he was identified. As a member of the church, a man of affairs, and as a politician, he was always active, considerate and progressive, and during his long and busy life great scope has been given to his rare business and executive ability. Everywhere he was recognized as a man of probity and honor. It has been the privilege of but few men to be in touch with so many business interests, so many public matters and so many people as he. In every phase of life he was found to be an exemplary man, and in whatever business he was engaged, and whatever public trust was committed to him, he always proved to be able and progressive. He was a good citizen, and stood for all that was best in the life of the community.

What we know of his courtesy, sagacity, tact and good judgment as the President of the Morning Bulletin Company every concern knows with which he has had close business relations. He was a pillar of strength to any concern.

As the Mayor of the city of Norwich for a period of ten years he gave a large part of his time to public business, and as chairman ex-officio of the committees of the Court of Common Council he became thoroughly familiar with all the details of public business, and acquired such an amount of information and such an interest in city affairs that it has never waned since his retirement from office in 1886. From that time to this he has been the adviser of every mayor of the city, be he democrat or republican, in many matters of importance, and it has been conceded that Norwich never had a more capable or faithful citizen in the mayor's chair.

Those familiar only with his business life have little conception of his warm-heartedness and amiability in social life. And this warm side was not kept exclusively for his friends. His ear and heart were open to the unfortunate, as well as the fortunate, and he was a liberal contributor to many worthy persons and all good work. His broadness was shown by the fact that men of all faiths, all parties and all kinds of business sought his advice and received it, and his worth to the community is made clear by the frank expressions of sorrow and regret which today come from the people because of the ending of his long, useful and successful career.

Windham County Transcript.

Mr. Osgood, whose death the papers recorded last Monday, was a man of rare parts. He had most of the

47

characteristics that make men as nearly perfect as they can be in a world where perfection is never reached. He was excellent on almost all lines. He lived in the open, having nothing to disguise or hide. He was a professed Christian and he honored his profession. He was a philanthropist, and he gave not to be seen of men, but to benefit the sharers in his free bounty. He was a business man that had the interests of his customers at heart as well as his own. He was a politician, not for personal honor, but to advance what he felt was right. He was a husband because he wanted a home with all that word means, and he, with another, is said to have made it as near an ideal as earthly homes ever are. Last, but not least, he was trusted because he deserved to be and because no one was ever disappointed who put trust in him.

Such men are of immense value. They set examples, and while many will not follow in their footsteps, some will, and all ought to.

Mr. Osgood had large money interests in Windham County, and no one who ever knew him intimately but will sorrow that they " will see his face no more."

Bridgeport Telegram.

In the death of ex-Mayor Hugh H. Osgood, Norwich loses a staunch champion. Mayor Osgood stood all the time for Norwich, was liberal to the fullest degree and counted his friends by the thousands. His popularity was not confined to Norwich, by any means. He was respected by all who knew him. The loss is Connecticut's.

Eastern Connecticut Churchman.

The death of Col. H. H. Osgood ends a record of a well-spent life, and takes from this community a character singularly well-rounded out and complete in all that goes to make up the ideal of age and experience. With a placid demeanor and a courtly manner he handled wisely so many great interests that it was a marvel, not only how he could give them his thought and attention, but how he could do so with apparently so little of mental disturbance.

His quiet force of character was seen in all he did. No one knows, or ever will know until the great day of accounts, his numerous acts of unostentatious generosity. Many, on the other hand, will hold him in continual remembrance for many kind offices, his unfailing interest in all that was good, his untiring work for the well-being of his fellowmen, whether in their individual or corporate capacity. His wise counsel, in almost countless cases, has been the means of helping many over apparently insurmountable difficulties. He was a good friend to St. Andrew's Church. May perpetual light shine upon him!

Hartford Courant.

The death of Colonel Hugh H. Osgood, of Norwich, takes out of the affairs of that city and the state one of their best citizens. Mr. Osgood was 78 years old but still alert and interested as he had been for so many years. He was mayor of Norwich for ten years, and has held innumerable positions of trust there. His name was synonymous with integrity and public spirit. Everybody trusted him and he deserved their confidence. For many years he was a great political power in that part of Connecticut, and he used his large influence in a broad and honorable way. He was the sort of a man that makes a community better by being a part of it.

Extracts from Letters.

We all mourn the loss. We respected, honored, admired, loved him. It is good to have known such a man.

A. D. G.

It always seemed to me he was one who would always be with us; one we could not possibly spare.

E. F. G.

How much Mr. Osgood will be missed in the community. We never can see a time ripe to spare so good a man.

L. L. A.

His worth was known far and wide. He was known to be a true man, and his place cannot well be filled in Norwich.

Mrs. L. A. H.

Mr. Osgood was one of the best men that ever lived. He commanded great respect and liking wherever he was known. How he will be missed in Norwich.

M. E. W.

51

Mr. Osgood has been a good friend to me, and I shall always remember with sincere gratitude his kindness and helpfulness.   R. S. R.

We feel ourselves what a great loss has come to us, and what a true, reliable, disinterested friend and counsellor we have no longer left to go to for advice.

J. H. W.

A strong, true hearted, honest souled man has gone out of Norwich, and all the region must feel the loss as long as any are left who remember him.   E. R. C.

I make the strong assertion that the district and, in fact, the whole city feel their loss to be well nigh irreparable.   Such tributes are due and paid to but few men, for but few have been so worthy.   C. B. W.

I will not harrow your feelings by writing all the beautiful things about Cousin H. I could write, which we all know and appreciate, and which will be a sweet memory of an ideal life passed away in its full worth.

L. O. W.

I shall never forget Thursday, and the wonderful and universal recognition of what he was is a most inspiring memory.   It is surely an incentive to every one for renewed effort in contemplating such a beautiful life.

E. J.

He was so cordial and kind to me; his life so noble, one could not come in contact with him without being better. It has always been such a source of pleasure to have known him.   G. R. L.

I want to tell you how personal an affliction we feel it to be. Mr. Osgood was such a loyal friend and neighbor that his passing away is a distinct loss to us and to the entire community.   H. C. A.

Let me tell you how deeply and sincerely I share the grief of so many in the death of your husband. It seems a loss that can never be replaced ; a loss in so very many ways his death is for his friends, and for the city no common sorrow, but a great bereavement.

Miss C. T.

I cannot tell you how we have felt for you in your loss. Mr. Osgood had a warmer spot in our hearts than we have ever expressed, and his many unspeakable kindnesses we can never forget. I only wish he might have known what was too hard to put into words.

H. R. T.

With neither wish nor willingness to intrude upon your sorrow in view of the irreparable loss which has come to you and our community by the death of your honored husband, I cannot forbear this expression of my affectionate sympathy and my own sense of personal bereavement in the death of my life friend.   E. N. G.

I need not tell you of the lifelong friendship that existed between Colonel Osgood and my father. There was no one whom he so highly honored and loved. Where are the men who can fill the place made vacant by the death of one like your husband?

A. P. C.

It is truly a great loss, first of all to you, but also to the many who have known him intimately, and to some of us who have seen him seldom but have respected and admired him greatly. It has always been a pleasure to me since my visit to you to recall his gracious, kindly manner and his altogether charming personality.

M. L. D.

His loved and honored friend for many years, my father feels the great loss all the more keenly in that he met Mr. Osgood daily in his business life, and relied on him for the good counsel which was never failing. Every one feels that they are sharing a sorrow common to all Norwich, and their sincere sympathy is with you.

M. V. C.

We found (on our arrival in Turkey) papers conveying the sad news of Mr. Osgood's death and the many resolutions, etc. What a grand showing for a long life. I remember when I first met Colonel Osgood at the Vendome, how impressed I was with him as one of the best of the New England type. It was truly so, and will ennoble all your after life to have the memory of such a husband. We all saw how happy was your home life.

L. O. L.

We little thought when we parted from you in Norwich that Mr. Osgood was so near the end of his earthly life. Mr. L. and I conceived a very strong admiration for Mr. Osgood during our acquaintance with him. He was certainly a rare man among men, and Norwich will not often see his like. One could not be with him without conceiving a powerful impression of his nobility, his sincerity and uprightness, clear judgment; his deep, Christian character, his kindliness, geniality and sympathy towards all. He was so young in spirit.

Mrs. C. H. L.

I had known the Colonel nearly twenty-five years; and as time went on had learned to respect and esteem him very highly and to value his friendship more and more as I found how true it was, and I know that in his decease I have lost a tried and true friend. The spontaneous and universal tokens of respect shown his memory by the large and impressive gathering to perform the last sad rites on Thursday told more eloquently than words can how deeply his loss is regretted by the community which was the scene of his life's work; and that his worth and sterling integrity are thus recognized must be a consolation to his friends.   T. F. M.

If all men were like him, what a world this would be; and does it not show that after all a man who has character, truth and perfect integrity is appreciated and the world will honor and appreciate it. There is a comfort in feeling that he was taken in the prime of his usefulness. How happy you made him. It was your care and watchfulness which gave him comfort and a prolonged life. What splendid resolutions have been passed, from the heart—no mere form, the tolling of the bell, a whole community in tears; it is all so touching, so wonderful. He is gone! I can hardly make myself believe it. Never more to meet his warm greeting, his bright smile and the laughing twinkle of his eye.   M. S. J.

From Business Associates.

Mr. Osgood has been associated with me as stockholder and director for thirty-six years. We shall miss his good judgment and excellent ability.   J. O. S.

Of the Company your husband was an honorary member, and a very much endeared one to us all. I regret inability to properly express our deep sorrow with you. Mr. Osgood was for many years active in the company, and at all times his interest in our welfare was keen and alive to our best interests. We all feel that we have lost a good, tried and true friend, and the sympathy we feel for you cannot be expressed in words.   A. J. S.

Colonel Osgood was a true man, a true Christian man. He was a man of the highest integrity. His bond added nothing to his word. I have known him fifty years and have never known him to do a disonorable act. He sympathized with suffering and never refused deserving need. I honored and loved him, and deeply feel his loss. We have few men left who are like him.   J. M.

As a friend and neighbor in the highest ideal of those relations, Colonel Osgood's death is most sincerely regretted, and his memory most tenderly cherished. There is hardly a family in his neighborhood but has known him through some of those services which answer the question: Who is my neighbor? There are some, too, who went to him for advice in matters of personal or business perplexity, and who miss his sympathetic hearing of their difficulties, and his wise counsel given from his sound judgment and his warm heart. To one of these at least he stood in the place of the natural adviser who could no longer be consulted.

B. P. L.

A life like Colonel Osgood's makes its impression easily. It is inconceivable that any observer should miss the true estimate of his character. The simple, symmetrical lines upon which he lived and worked were before all men, and were unmistakable. They led in one parallel direction to the highest degree of nobility. There was no deviation from a high and honorable standard. It was born in him to be always noble and always true to a perfect manhood. There was no secret process by which he gained the esteem, the regard and the love of his fellow men. These returns fell to him like ripe fruit. He cultivated and nourished his natural ambition and ability as helper and adviser, and the harvest was his in maturity and completeness. His aim was usefulness, without show or pretension. He worked for results by the plainest, most direct and always honest methods. Sharp

58

or equivocal dealings to his sense of rectitude were intolerable. Where differences arose he was fearless, brave and chivalrous. All business transactions of his were sure to be without spot or blemish.

Not every one who knew him had the opportunity to note the natural order and conduct of his life. It was the fortune of a few to know him in *all* his proportions, not only as a friend, but as a reliant, forceful man of affairs, a wise counsellor and a loyal, sympathetic helper. The home community knew generally of his intense public spirit, which it seemed to expect of him as a matter of course. It knew something of his liberality, his benevolence and kindness of heart. It knew how he relieved, supported and befriended. A few realized that the pleasure of his life was to work and to do, not alone for himself, but as often for whomsoever stood in need. To every problem presented he gave the best energies that were in him. He shirked no responsibility. It was the grace and dignity of his bearing toward the people amongst whom he lived that led them to him for comfort and for aid. They knew him and they confided.

To speak of Col. Osgood's relations to me personally, or of mine to him, would be to invade a privacy I cannot touch upon. I can only inscribe my regret that any tribute of mine to his cherished name must be inadequate in expressing the loss of so dear and true a friend. There is great consolation in the remembrance of a close association with him through many years. It rests upon my heart like a benediction, "the noblest and gentlest memory of the world."   J. H. S.